The English Reading Tree

Keith Goodman

Reading Age for this book: 9+

The reading age for the series will vary but starts at seven

The English Reading Tree Series has been written for children aged seven and over. It is the perfect tool for parents to get their children into the habit of reading.

This book has been created to entertain and educate young minds and is packed with information and trivia and lots of authentic images that bring the topic alive.

There is a quiz at the end to test how much has been learned

TABLE OF CONTENTS

Introduction

The Vietnam War was part of the Cold War fought between the
USA and the Soviet Union (Russia). It was a long conflict that
claimed the lives of many soldiers and civilians and divided
Americans as to whether it was worth fighting.

The reasons why the war started in the first place are complicated and can be traced back to the 19th century when the country was under French rule.

Vietnam is a country that is situated in Southeast Asia. It became a French colony in 1877 but came under Japanese rule in World War Two.

With Japan and France fighting over who had control of Vietnam, the people of Vietnam were rightly fed up with foreign interference and started an independence movement.

This revolutionary movement faced the almost impossible task of establishing Vietnam as an independent country but succeeded in the end after years of bitter fighting and negotiations.

This is the story of the Vietnam War.

The Countdown to War

1887 seems a long way to go back but go back we must. The French colonized Vietnam and named it Indochina.

After being trained by the Russians, Ho Chi Minh founded the Indochinese Communist Party in **1930**.

The French could do nothing to stop the Japanese invasion of Indochina in **1940**. Japanese troops were now in control.

In **August 1945,** the Americans, British and colonial forces defeated the Japanese in World War Two. Indochina was free of Japan, but the French tried to regain control.

In **September 1945**, Ho Chi Minh declared North Vietnam independent of French rule. Despite modeling his new republic's declaration on the USA Declaration of Independence, America did not support him.

In **January 1950**, both the Soviet Union (communist Russia) and communist China recognized the communist Democratic Republic of Vietnam. They started to supply Vietnam with military and economic aid.

March-May 1954 saw France humiliated by Ho Chi Minh's forces at the Battle of Dien Bien Phu. The French had lost heart in the fight and looked for a way out of Vietnam.

There was a famous speech by the American President, Dwight D. Eisenhower, in **April 1954**. In the speech, the president outlined the dangers of communist control of countries in Asia. He called it the domino effect. America became obsessed with trying to stop the spread of communism.

The Geneva Accords in **July 1954** split Vietnam into North Vietnam and South Vietnam. The dividing line was the 17th parallel. Under this agreement, elections had to be held within two years to unify the country under on democratic government.

1955 saw North Vietnam under the communist rule of Ho Chi Minh and South Vietnam under the American-backed control of leader, Ngo Dinh Diem.

Ho Chi Minh was not satisfied with Vietnam being split into two. In **1959,** North Vietnamese guerrilla forces began to attack the

South. They use a trail through Cambodia and Laos. This became known to the world as the Ho Chi Minh Trail.

US soldiers were killed in South Vietnam in **July 1959**.

America began to drift slowly into a full-blown war.

The Battle of Dien Bien Phu

French prisoners being escorted by Vietnamese troops

The Battle of Dien Bien Phu made the French Government concede that it had lost control of its colony.

French troops had occupied the Dien Bien Phu valley in 1953 and seemed to have miscalculated the strength of the Vietnamese forces (Viet Minh).

The battle started in March and ended in May with thousands of French soldiers taken prisoner. Communist China backed up the Viet

Minh. The loss of the French airfield meant that getting supplies into the area became difficult.

The French eventually surrendered, and the French Government signed the Geneva Accords in 1954, which ended the fighting and French involvement in Vietnam (Indochina).

The Ho Chi Minh Trail

Often bicycles were used on the trail to transport munitions

The Ho Chi Minh Trail was a supply track that started in North Vietnam and crossed into Laos and Cambodia before arriving in South Vietnam.

The North Vietnamese sent ammunition and weapons down the trail.

Soldiers also used it as a means of crossing the border to carry out guerrilla raids.

The trail got its name from the President of North Vietnam, Ho Chi Minh.

The trail was not just one path but a collection of tracks joined together to allow tons of equipment to be transported very quickly.

It went through dense jungle and high mountains.

The original trail started near the capital city of North Vietnam, Hanoi, and ran 1000 miles to the capital of South Vietnam, Saigon.

Vietnam War Timeline 1960 to 1963

In **September 1960**, Le Duan took over as the head of the North Vietnamese communist party. Ho Chi Minh had health problems but still maintained an influence.

The National Liberation Front (NLF) was started in **December 1960**, in South Vietnam, with the backing of the North Vietnamese. The NLF was a communist anti-government political party.

In **May 1961,** the US President John F Kennedy sent helicopters and troops to Vietnam to fight the North Vietnamese. The 400 Green Berets operated in secrecy.

Operation Ranch Hand started in **January 1962**. American planes began spraying a deadly chemical called Agent Orange over the jungle. The aim was to destroy vegetation, which the North Vietnamese soldiers were using as cover.

In **February 1962**, the South Vietnamese leader, Ngo Dinh Diem, survived an assassination attempt.

The village of Ap Bac, situated near Saigon, was the scene of a humiliating defeat for South Vietnamese soldiers in **January 1963**. A much smaller North Vietnamese force defeated them.

The USA had grown tired of the corrupt Ngo Dinh Diem and unofficially backed his removal from power in **November 1963**. There was political chaos in South Vietnam as various factions fought for control in the aftermath.

JF Kennedy was assassinated in Dallas also in **November 1963**, and the new President, Lyndon B Johnson was sworn into power.

The National Liberation Front

Viet Cong guerrillas

The National Front for the Liberation of South Vietnam was formed out of several political parties that were not very happy with the rule of South Vietnamese President Ngo Dinh Diem. Although dominated by communists, the NLF had non-communist and religious groups under its banner. They were nicknamed the Viet Cong by the Americans.

The military section of the NLF (National Liberation Front) was the PLAF or People's Liberation Armed Forces.

After an attack by the PLAF in 1965, President Lyndon B Johnson sent in American ground troops to help support the South Vietnamese.

Operation Ranch Hand

American planes spraying defoliating chemicals on the Vietnamese forests

The American Air Force launched an operation called Ranch Hand to stop the PLAF's movement and expose secret trails in the jungle.

It is estimated that around 19 million gallons of defoliating herbicides were used over about 20 percent of Vietnam and parts of Laos between 1962 and 1971.

The most frequent chemical used was, the deadly, Agent Orange (named after the orange containers).

This chemical destroyed the jungle but didn't stop the North Vietnamese.

The long-term ecological impact of using Agent Orange and its side effects on humans was one of the big controversial arguments about the Vietnam War.

Agent Orange caused health problems like skin rashes, cancer, and birth disabilities.

Ngo Dinh Diem

Ngo Dinh Diem was a fiercely Catholic Vietnamese politician who took control of South Vietnam, after the Geneva Accords, in July 1955. The USA and other anti-communist countries backed him.

There was discontent against his rule, which was growing as the Viet Cong (PLAF) became stronger. His persecution of Vietnam's Buddhists would be the final straw that turned the USA against him. His violence against Buddhists led to a military coup and his assassination by generals in the South Vietnamese Army. It was widely known that the Americans secretly backed this military revolution.

Ngo Dinh Diem's regime was considered very corrupt, and he was thought to be no more than a puppet dictator controlled by America.

Vietnam War Timeline 1964 to 1965

In **August 1964**, the USS Maddox was allegedly attacked by a North Vietnamese torpedo boat in the Gulf of Tonkin. US President Johnson ordered reprisal airstrikes on torpedo boat bases.

The American Congress authorized the Gulf of Tonkin Resolution. This was a resolution that meant the US President could use any measures necessary against North Vietnam or any other enemy involved in the conflict.

The Soviet (Russian) Politburo sent weapons, food, and medical support to North Vietnam in **November 1964**. Communist China also sent troops.

Operation Flaming Dart commenced in **1965**. It was authorized by President Johnson and targeted North Vietnam. It was an aerial operation that targeted North Vietnamese military bases.

Operation Rolling Thunder commenced in **March 1965**. It was a three-year campaign of bombing strategic targets in North Vietnam and along the Ho Chi Minh Trail. US Marines landed in Vietnam.

Military leader General Nguen Van Thieu became president of South Vietnam in **June 1965**.

The US sent 50,000 troops to Vietnam in July **1965**.

The first big ground offensive by the Americans took place in **August 1965**. Over 5,000 US Marines engaged with the North Vietnamese in a six-day battle called Operation Starlight.

In **November 1965**, many American troops were killed or injured in the Battle of La Drang Valley.

Gulf of Tonkin Incident

The USS Maddox

In 1964, the situation in Vietnam was dictated by America's policy of stopping the spread of communism. The support of South Vietnam became more formalized after the attack on two American warships in the Gulf of Tonkin. The USS Maddox and the USS Turner Joy were in the Gulf of Tonkin to support South Vietnamese raids on North Vietnam.

Both ships reported that they had been fired upon by North Vietnamese Patrol boats, and because of this, the US Congress passed the Gulf of Tonkin Resolution.

This resolution gave American President Lyndon Johnson the power to use all necessary measures to stop attacks against the forces of the USA. It was passed in August 1964.

In 2005 and 2006, classified military documents were released that suggested that the attacks on the warships that escalated the USA's involvement in Vietnam were exaggerated. The war would become very unpopular with Americans and led to many protests.

Operation Rolling Thunder

America started this bombing campaign in March 1965. The aerial attacks on North Vietnam were designed to destroy military targets, discourage the North Vietnamese from continuing the war, and boost the morale of South Vietnamese. There was also bombing of the Ho Chi Minh Trail to stop or at least limit supplies being sent into the South

Initially, Operation Rolling Thunder targeted areas close to the north/south border, but this gradually moved further into North Vietnam. By the spring of 1966, planes attacked industrial and military targets all over the North.

As Rolling Thunder gained momentum, US ground forces arrived to defend American airbases in South Vietnam. Their mission was soon expanded also to engage with the North Vietnamese in combat. These troop numbers gradually increased throughout the 1960s.

The North Vietnamese Air Force was not very big. Instead of engaging America in the air, the North developed an excellent air defense system with the help of Russia and China. They shot down hundreds of American planes and captured a lot of American pilots and crew.

A bit like the attack on Pearl Harbor that unified America against Japan, the bombing raids unified the North Vietnamese against the Americans and were used as propaganda to influence international public opinion.

The continual bombing of the North lasted for over three years and finally ended in October 1968.

Operation Starlight

This was the first major battle involving almost entirely American troops. The battle also is known as the Battle of Van Tuong. It lasted from the 18th to the 24th of August 1965 and is considered a victory to the USA.

The American Marines were supported by gunfire from US Navy warships off the coast and inflicted heavy casualties on the North Vietnamese Army.

This was the first major battle that saw the Americans on the offensive and not just deployed to defend airbases. Although both sides claimed victory, the American casualties were far less than the reported North Vietnamese casualties.

The Battle of La Drang Valley

The Battle of la Drang Valley was another significant encounter that saw American troops take on North Vietnamese forces. The battle started on November 14, 1965.

The 1st Battalion of the 7th Cavalry attacked with helicopters and was soon fighting the North Vietnamese 33rd Regiment. The battle continued all day and into the night.

The US forces were supported by airstrikes and shelling from nearby artillery units.

The next day the Vietnamese 66th Regiment joined in the battle.

It took three days of fierce fighting for the American troops to gain the upper hand.

Although North Vietnamese casualties were heavy, American losses were also high.

This battle showed that the North Vietnamese were willing to fight battles as well as use guerrilla tactics.

American commanders thought that engaging in battle with North Vietnamese troops could be a road to victory.

The North Vietnamese concluded that if they fought with Americans at close quarters, this would stop airstrikes because the Americans would be afraid of attacking their own troops.

Vietnam War Timeline 1966 to 1967

In **1966,** the number of American troops in Vietnam rose to 400,000.

The American Air Force attacked targets in Haiphong and Hanoi in June **1966**.

By **1967** the number of American troops in Vietnam had risen to 500,000

In **February 1967**, the US Air Force attacked Haiphong Harbour and other North Vietnamese airfields.

There were massive protests against the war in San Francisco, New York City, and Washington in **April 1967**.

Nguyen Van Thieu won the presidential election in South Vietnam in **September 1967**.

In **November 1967,** there was an offensive in the Vietnamese Central Highlands by North Vietnamese troops. The Battle of Dak-To saw US and South Vietnamese forces under attack.

The Battle of Dak-To

The Battle of Dak-To was one of the fiercest of the war and occurred in the Central Highlands of Vietnam. It took place in November 1967. There were about 4,500 US and South Vietnamese troops that faced around 6,000 North Vietnamese soldiers of the 174th regiment. After intense fighting, the North Vietnamese withdrew with heavy losses.

The reason for the battle was because of the determination of the North to clear the area of American forces. This is an area where the borders of South Vietnam, Cambodia, and Laos meet.

The North targeted the Special Forces camps at Ben Het and Dak-To. These camps were causing problems to the North's ability to get arms down the Ho Chi Minh Trail.

The terrain of this area is about as hostile as it can get. The heavily packed jungle made it difficult to move around and is full of deadly snakes and mosquitoes. It was described by American troops as Hell on Earth.

Anti War Protests

Anti-war protests in Amsterdam in 1966

The protests against the Vietnam War began slowly on University

campuses, but support among Americans grew as the USA

committed more troops.

In 1967, around half a million American troops were in Vietnam,

and casualties and deaths were reported daily to the American public

on TV. The war was costing billions of dollars. The protests against

the war joined together Americans from various backgrounds who

wanted to see America pull out.

The draft system in the USA meant that as many as 40,000 young Americans a month were forced to join the armed forces. Many crossed the border into Canada to avoid having to go to Asia and fight. Many Americans had never even heard of Vietnam before the war began, and lots didn't have a clue where the country was or why America was fighting a war there.

The war joined grieving families, university students, and many more sections of American society who all wanted an end to the deaths on both sides.

In October 1967, there were over 100,000 protesters gathered at the Lincoln Memorial in Washington DC. Many of the protestors marched to the Pentagon, and hundreds were arrested.

In 1967, the civil rights leader Martin Luther King Jr spoke of his opposition to the Vietnam War and called for funds spent on the war to be spent on domestic problems.

Far from going away, the protesting got stronger and influenced America's hand to start peace negotiations. The antiwar feeling was not just in the USA, and there were protests in many major cities around the world.

Vietnam War Timeline 1968 to 1969

From **January to April 1968**, the US Marine Garrison at Khe Sanh in South Vietnam was attacked with artillery shells by the People's Army of North Vietnam (PAVN). The attack lasted 77 days.

The Tet Offensive started in **January 1968**, and targeted more than 100 cities and other locations across South Vietnam, which included the capital city of Saigon.

The week ending the **17th of February 1968** had the highest number of American deaths. There were 543.

February to **March 1968** saw battles at Saigon and Hue that ended with an American victory.

The US massacre of 500 civilians at Mai Lai occurred in **March 1968**. The incident happened during a US search and destroy mission.

In **March 1968**, US President Johnson stopped bombing north of the 20th parallel and said he would not run for re-election.

Richard Nixon won the presidential election in **November 1968**.

In **May 1969**, US paratroopers attacked North Vietnamese troops near the Laos border. The fighting was so fierce it was called Hamburger Hill by the US newspapers.

Ho Chi Minh had a heart attack and died in September **1969**.

The Battle of Khe Sanh

The American base at Khe Sanh

The Battle of Khe Sanh started in January 1968. The PAVN (People's Army of North Vietnam) begun to shell the American Marine base near the Vietnamese border with Laos. The Americans and South Vietnamese fought off a savage attack that lasted for the next 77 days.

This was one of the most prolonged and fiercely fought battles of the war.

There were around 6,000 soldiers stationed at Khe Sanh, and they had orders to hold the base at all costs.

The American Air Force carried out airstrikes against suspected PAVN positions.

The base was eventually relieved in March by a combined Army and Marine task force, and the defense was considered a victory for the Americans. However, soon after the victory, the Americans dismantled the base and left, saying it was no longer needed. Because of this, the PAVN also claimed a victory, even though they had more casualties than the Marines.

The Tet Offensive

The US Embassy in Saigon was the scene of an attack

This was a highly organized attack by the North Vietnamese on cities and settlements around South Vietnam. The aim was to get the people of the South to rise up against the government and compel America to scale down its forces.

The offensive did not overrun the South Vietnamese and the Americans, and many North Vietnamese were killed or captured.

However, the publicity that the offensive received worldwide and in the USA turned public opinion even more against the war.

The Tet holiday is a celebration of the New Year and is the most celebrated holiday in Vietnam.

The holiday was so important that an informal truce was often held between fighting North and South forces.

January 31, 1968, was chosen by the North to start the Tet offensive. It started early on the morning of the 30th of January 1968 when the North Vietnamese launched attacks on 13 cities in the South. The attacks escalated to other towns and military bases over South Vietnam.

In Saigon, the PAVN attacked and entered the US Embassy. They were eventually driven away, but it was an event that shocked the American public. The North Vietnamese forces were not strong enough for an overall victory in the offensive, and the US and South Vietnamese were victorious and killed or wounded many of the enemy.

Even though the Tet offensive was not a success in a military sense, it was immense as a public relations exercise. The American President told the US public that the end of the war was in sight, but Tet showed that it was nowhere near a conclusion, and the North was far from beaten.

Tet turned out to be the catalyst turning point of the war.

Ho Chi Minh

A young Ho Chi Minh in France (1921)

Ho Chi Minh became a communist while he was living in France

during the First World War. He went to Russia and later helped start the Indochinese Communist Party and the League for the Independence of Vietnam.

After seizing control of North Vietnam and with Hanoi as its capital city, he became a symbol of the struggle to unify North and South.

He died of a heart attack on September 2, 1967. He was 79 years of age and didn't see the end of the war and the North's victory.

Hamburger Hill

After the conflict

The Battle of Hamburger Hill was fought over 10 days in May 1969. Hill 937 is in the intense jungle near the Vietnamese border with Laos. Even though the hill was not of tactical importance to the American Military, it was part of a larger campaign designed to inflict damage on the North Vietnamese Army.

On May 10, American paratroopers fought with the PAVN but were not successful and had to withdraw.

The North Vietnamese Regiment dug in on the hill consisted of many hardened veterans of the Tet campaign, and the battle was intense. The Americans were also backed up with airstrikes. At times, the battle was fought in torrential tropical rain so heavy that visibility was zero.

Because of the ferociousness of the battle to capture the hill and the number of casualties on both sides, the journalists covering the war nicknamed it Hamburger Hill. Like stepping into a hamburger machine.

When extra American and South Vietnamese troops arrived on May 20, the hill was taken, and the North Vietnamese retreated to the relative safety of Laos.

The hill was abandoned by American and South Vietnamese forces on June 5 because there was no reason to stay. The PAVN retook it in July.

Hamburger Hill started a storm of criticism in the USA because of the pointlessness of fighting a battle that had no meaning.

Vietnam War Timeline 1970 to 1972

After US President Richard Nixon started to reduce American troop numbers in Vietnam, secret peace talks began in **February 1970**.

Between **April and June 1970**, US and South Vietnamese forces crossed the border into Cambodia to attack PAVN bases.

The Kent State shooting took place on **May 4, 1970**.

In **June 1970,** the Gulf of Tonkin Resolution was canceled.

Between **January and March 1972**, Operation Lam Son saw United States and South Vietnamese troops enter Laos in an attempt to block the Ho Chi Minh Trail.

Between **March and October 1972**, the North Vietnamese Army went on the offensive and gained more land in South Vietnam.

Operation Linebacker was an intense bombing campaign against North Vietnam that started in **1972**.

Secret Peace Negotiations

Henry Kissinger

Henry Kissinger, the US National Security Adviser, began secret peace negotiations with North Vietnam in Paris in February 1970. The North Vietnamese representative was a high-ranking official named Le Duc Tho.

Le Duc Tho wanted an unconditional withdrawal of US forces in Vietnam.

Kissinger wanted a mutual withdrawal from the South, and for Cambodia to become neutral. He also wanted an electoral commission to supervise elections in South Vietnam.

Both sides were too far apart for an agreement.

An unconditional withdrawal would have implied that the war had been a mistake. The US leadership was looking for peace with dignity.

The Kent State Shootings

Anti-war protests in the USA and around the world continued in 1970. On May 4, 1970, soldiers from the Ohio National Guard shot into a crowd of student protestors at Kent State University. Four were killed, and nine other students were wounded.

The students were part of a 300 strong protest against America's expansion of the war into Vietnam's neighbor, Cambodia.

This incident caused mass outrage in universities all over the country, and over 4 million students took part in organized strikes in protest.

Public opinion against the Vietnam War continued to grow.

The Easter Offensive

Captured North Vietnamese Tank

The Nixon administration had reduced the number of American forces in Vietnam and placed more emphasis on South Vietnamese forces defending themselves. From around 550,000 military personnel in 1969, by 1972, there were approximately 70,000.

In March 1972, the North Vietnamese started the Easter Offensive with multiple attacks on South Vietnam.

The North Vietnamese troops were very well equipped with tanks and artillery supplied by China and Russia. This was the biggest offensive of the war, and it was against a dwindling number of American forces.

American military advisers helped the South Vietnamese Army and US air support successfully held back the invading forces.

The North Vietnamese Army sustained heavy losses, and much of its equipment was either destroyed or taken.

The offensive left over a million homeless, and casualties on both sides were high.

Operation Linebacker

An American B52 lands after completing a bombing mission

This was a combined US and South Vietnam operation to cut off supplies for the Easter Offensive by the North Vietnamese Army. It was the first continuous bombing attack to take place since Operation Rolling Thunder in 1968.

Operation Linebacker 2 was another intense bombing campaign over 12 days in December. The plan was to destroy targets in Hanoi and Haiphong in North Vietnam and was carried out by US Air Force B52s. The 12 days saw the biggest heavy bomber strikes carried out by America since the Second World War.

Linebacker 1 had caused devastation in the north and halted the Easter Offensive. It was enough pressure to convince the North Vietnamese Government to return to the Paris Peace table and make concessions to its demands. In return, the Americans ordered a halt to the bombing, and Kissinger announced that peace was close in Vietnam.

The difficult nature of negotiations in Paris led to the peace talks breaking down again as the South Vietnamese President, Thieu, made significant alterations to the document agreed by Kissinger and the North Vietnamese.

Hanoi negotiators walked away from the peace talks in December, and there was no date given to reconvene.

Kissinger's talks of peace had given the American public false hope. The American President, Richard Nixon, wanted to bring the

North Vietnamese Government back to Paris, so he started bombing again (Operation Linebacker 2).

The North agreed to come back to the peace negotiations in Paris, and Operation Linebacker 2 was halted.

The aftermath of the bombing saw the government of North Vietnam complaining that the Americans had attacked hospitals, schools, and heavily populated residential areas.

Not only China and Russia denounced the bombing. The Prime Minister of Sweden made a speech condemning Linebacker. In response, America cut off diplomatic relations with Sweden.

Vietnam War Timeline 1973

At the age of 64, the former US President, Johnson, died on **January 22, 1973**.

On **January 27, 1973**, the draft came to an end. The US military was now manned by volunteers

On **January 27, 1973**, US President, Richard Nixon, signed the Paris Peace Accords. This ended America's direct involvement in the war. Even though North Vietnam accepted a ceasefire, the USA was concerned that North Vietnamese plans were still in place to invade the South.

North Vietnam returned 591 US prisoners of war between **February and April 1973**.

The Paris Peace Accords

Signing the peace agreement

The peace agreement to end the war was signed by South Vietnam, North Vietnam, and the USA on January 27, 1973. The peace talks also included the Republic of South Vietnam (Viet Cong), who were the representatives of the South Vietnamese Communists.

The main terms of the agreement:

- US troops to leave Vietnam

- The return of prisoners of war

- Clearing mines from North Vietnam's ports by the Americans

- A cease-fire in South Vietnam

- The organization of free elections in South Vietnam under neutral supervision

- The reunification of Vietnam by peaceful means

- Foreign troops to withdraw from Cambodia and Laos.

- US financial help to restore the area

The Peace Accords removed the USA from the conflict in Vietnam, but the conflict didn't stop. The North and the South continued to ignore much of the agreement. North Vietnam continued to build up its military power for a strike against the South, but the South would not have any help from America this time.

Vietnam War Timeline 1974 to 1975

In **August 1974**, the Watergate scandal rocked the USA, and US President, Richard Nixon, resigned to be replaced by Gerald R. Ford.

In **January 1975**, even though fighting had continued in Vietnam, President Ford would not commit America to help.

Without American help, it was only a matter of time, and Saigon fell to communist forces in **April 1975**.

In July 1975, North and South Vietnam became one country. The Socialist Republic of Vietnam.

The Fall of Saigon

Vietnamese refugees land by helicopter on an American warship

The capital city of South Vietnam, Saigon, was captured by the People's Army of Vietnam and the Viet Cong on April 30, 1975. The South Vietnamese forces collapsed under the pressure of the attack.

Even though there had been vague promises of support by the USA, with the Watergate Scandal, no help was given, and Nixon was impeached and lost the presidency. His successor Gerald Ford did not want to pick up the poison chalice of sending troops back to Vietnam.

The North Vietnamese eventually encircled Saigon, and the South Vietnamese President, Nguyen Van Thieu, resigned and fled.

The attack on Saigon was an anticlimax, as by then, there was no resistance left.

Before the fall, US Marine and Air Force helicopters rescue 1,000 American civilians and around 7,000 South Vietnamese refugees in a mad 18-hour evacuation of the city.

Facts and Figures of the Vietnam War

About 2,700,000 Americans served in uniform during the Vietnam War

58,148 Americans were killed in Vietnam, with thousands more disabled or partially disabled

About 75 percent of the US military serving in Vietnam were volunteers.

The average age of an American infantryman in Vietnam was 22 (not 19)

The Vietnam War was lost by the South Vietnamese. The fall of Saigon happened two years after the Americans had officially left. The fall of Saigon was April 30, 1975. The last American soldier left Vietnam on March 29, 1973.

Saigon is now called Ho Chi Minh City.

The capital city of Vietnam is Hanoi.

In Vietnam, the war is known as the Resistance War against America, or simply the American War.

The Vietnam War was fought between South Vietnam and North Vietnam. The USA was the ally of South Vietnam, and the Soviet Union and China supported North Vietnam. It was part of the Cold War (proxy war) between the Soviet Union and the western powers.

It is believed that up to 4 million people lost their lives because of the war. This included military personnel and civilians.

The Vietnam War cost the USA over one trillion dollars in today's money

Over 400,000 troops from other nations served in Vietnam:

- South Korea sent 320,000 soldiers and was the most committed ally of the USA.

- Australia sent over 61,000 military personnel.

- The Philippines sent around 10,000 troops

- Around 4,000 troops from New Zealand fought in Vietnam

- Troops from Thailand were stationed in Vietnam during the war

- The fervent anti-communist government of Taiwan sent troops (special services) and transport planes.

- Canada helped with military supplies for the USA war effort. Some Canadians volunteered to fight.

- Although communist, Cuba was never officially part of the war; it probably did have a small presence on the side of the north.

There was bitter resentment in the USA about the deaths of American soldiers. Over 58,000 Americans died. However, 2 million Vietnamese civilians died and around 1.5 million soldiers. This puts American deaths at less than 2 percent.

The AK-47 used by the North Vietnamese was statistically a far more reliable rifle than the M16 used by American troops. The M16 tended to jam because of mud and dust.

In 1964, young men started to burn their draft cards to protest against the war. Although this was, illegal not many protestors were arrested for doing it.

Post War Vietnam

Ho Chi Minh City (Saigon)

The capital city is Hanoi

The population of Vietnam is 96,462,106.

The country is slightly bigger than New Mexico.

Vietnam shares borders with Laos, Cambodia, and China and is situated in Southeast Asia

Climate

Tropical in the North and subtropical in the South and Center.
The rainy season is between May and September.

Cities

- Ho Chi Minh City has over 5 million inhabitants

- Hanoi has 2.6 million people

- Haiphong has 2 million people

- Da Nang has a population of 900,000

Even though many Vietnamese live in the countryside, there have been many that have moved to the major cities of Hanoi and Ho Chi Minh City.

Like most countries, the Vietnamese enjoy sport, especially soccer, volleyball, table tennis, and martial arts.

Vietnam is still a communist state and has an expanding economy and a very healthy tourist industry.

Vietnam War Quiz

1 Which European country colonized Vietnam in 1877?

2 What was the capital city of North Vietnam?

3 What was the name of the trail that ran from North Vietnam, through Laos to South Vietnam?

4 What was the name of the North Vietnamese Campaign that attacked cities in South Vietnam in January 1968?

5 What was the name of the American National Security Adviser that started secret peace talks with North Vietnam in 1970?

6 In which European cities did the peace talks take place?

7 Which US President signed the Peace Accords?

8 What year did Vietnam become one country?

Thank you for Reading this Book

You can visit the English Reading Tree Page by clicking:

<u>Visit Amazon's Keith Goodman Page</u> (Mailing List)

Books in the English Reading Tree Series by Keith Goodman include:

1 The Titanic for Kids

2 Shark Facts for Kids

3 Solar System Facts for Kids

4 Dinosaur Facts for Kids

5 American Facts and Trivia for Kids

6 Christmas Facts and Trivia for Kids

7 Space Race Facts for Kids

8 My Titanic Adventure for Kids

9 Save the Titanic for Kids

10 Halloween Facts and Trivia for Kids

25 Planet Earth Explained for Kids

26 The Wild West and Stuff for Kids

27 The Great Depression and Stuff for Kids

28 Early American History for Kids

29 Awesome Alabama for Kids

30 Twentieth-Century America for Kids

31 American Democracy Explained for Kids

32 Amazing Alaska for Kids

33 All About Christmas for Kids

34 Christmas Parlor Games for Kids

35 America at War for Kids

36 Discovering Ancient Greece for Kids

37 The Vikings for Kids

38 The History of Ancient Weapons

53 The Russian Revolution Explained for Kids

54 America in the 1950s for Kids

55 America in the 1960s for Kids

56 UFO Mysteries for Kids

57 America in the 1970s for Kids

58 Ancient Mesopotamia for Kids

59 America in the 1980s for Kids

60 America in the 1940s for Kids

61 America in the 1990s for Kids

62 America in the 1930s for Kids

63 America in the 1920s for Kids

64 Chinese Dynasties for Kids for Kids

65 America from 1910 to 1919 for Kids

66 1917 for Kids

67 The Titanic Diary for Kids

68 Myths and Legends for Kids

69 The Loch Ness Monster for Kids

70 Ghost Stories for Kids

71 More UFO Stories for Kids

72 More Ghost Stories for Kids

73 The Planet Mars for Kids

74 The Planet Mercury for Kids

75 The Bigfoot Mystery for Kids

76 The Planet Venus for Kids

77 Unexplained Mysteries for Kids

78 The Planet Jupiter for Kids

79 The Planet Saturn for Kids

80 The Vietnam War for Kids

Other books by the same author:

Meet the Boneheads

The School Bully: Meet the Boneheads

Books From the For School Series

1 Native American History for School Grades 3 – 5

2 Colonial American History for School Grades 3 – 5

3 The American Revolution for School Grades 3 – 5

4 The American Industrial Revolution for School Grades 3 – 5

5 The American Civil War for School Grades 3 – 5

Other Books in the Living History Series

1 Ancient Britain for Kids

2 Roman Britain for kids

3 Anglo-Saxon Britain for Kids

4 Viking Britain for Kids

5 Norman Britain for Kids

6 Plantagenet England for Kids

7 Tudor England for Kids

8 17th Century England for Kids

9 Georgian Britain for Kids

10 Victorian Britain for Kids

11 Britain at War for Kids

12 World War Two Britain for Kids

Quiz Answers

1 France

2 Hanoi

3 The Ho Chi Minh Trail

4 The Tet Offensive

5 Henry Kissinger

6 Paris

7 Richard Nixon

8 1975

Attributions

Don-kun, NordNordWest, CC BY-SA 3.0
<https://creativecommons.org/licenses/by-sa/3.0>, via Wikimedia
Commons

Vietnam war 1957 to 1960 map english.svg

Author and licence can be found here

https://commons.wikimedia.org/wiki/File:Vietnam_war_1957_to_1960_
map_english.svg

Stringer, AFP, Public domain, via Wikimedia Commons

Dien Bien Phu 1954 French prisoners

Author and licence can be found here

https://commons.wikimedia.org/wiki/File:Dien_Bien_Phu_1954_Frenc
h_prisoners.jpg

Ron Kroon / Anefo, CC0, via Wikimedia Commons

Protestdemonstraties tegen oorlog in Vietnam, demonstranten met

leuzen, Bestanddeelnr 919-3118.jpg

Author and licence can be found here

Ho Chi Minh City Skyline

Author and licence can be found here

Made in United States
Orlando, FL
01 November 2022

24110251R00046